CLICK AND CLONE

OTHER BOOKS BY ELAINE EQUI

Ripple Effect: New & Selected Poems, 2007

The Cloud of Knowable Things, 2003

Voice-Over, 1998

Friendship with Things, 1998

Decoy, 1994

Surface Tension, 1989

Views without Rooms, 1989

Accessories, 1988

The Corners of the Mouth, 1986

Shrewcrazy, 1981

Federal Woman, 1978

Click and Clone

POEMS

ELAINE EQUI

COFFEE HOUSE PRESS
MINNEAPOLIS 2011

Coffee House Press books are available to the trade through our primary distributor, Consortium Book Sales & Distribution, www.cbsd.com or (800) 283-3572. For personal orders, catalogs, or other information, write to: info@coffeehousepress.org.

Coffee House Press is a nonprofit literary publishing house. Support from private foundations, corporate giving programs, government programs, and generous individuals helps make the publication of our books possible. We gratefully acknowledge their support in detail in the back of this book. To you and our many readers around the world, we send our thanks for your continuing support.

Good books are brewing at www.coffeehousepress.org

LIBRARY OF CONGRESS CATALOGING-IN-PUBLICATION DATA
Click and clone / by Elaine Equi.
p. cm.
ISBN 978-1-56689-257-5 (alk. paper)
I. Title.
PS3555.Q5C56 2011
811'.54—dc22
2010038006
Printed in the United States
1 3 5 7 9 8 6 4 2
FIRST EDITION | FIRST PRINTING

ACKNOWLEDGMENTS
Thanks to the editors of the following magazines where some of these poems first appeared: *Agriculture Reader, The American Poetry Review, Bald Ego, Barrow Street, Court Green, Denver Quarterly, Fou, Interval(le)s, Jacket, La Petite Zine, LIT, Margie, The Nation, Ocho, Otolith, Pax Americana, Peaches and Bats, Poetry, Pool, Puppy Flowers, Quarterly West, Tin House,* and *Vanitas.* "What Is It about Hands?" was included in *The Best American Poetry 2010,* edited by Amy Gerstler and David Lehman.

for the entity who goes by the name of
JEROME SALA

CONTENTS

FOLLOW ME

The flower breathes
the window's perfume.

The wall opens
its door.

I don't stay
inside the line.

I don't go
outside the line.

I am the line itself
which separates

one dreamy vacuum
from another.

I know better
than to go punching holes
in the universe.

Words float
in the balloon
above my head.

MANIFESTO

after Breton

When I dream, I vote.

Exercise my rights
as citizen of the dream state
to terra-form the future.

Work to abolish
the most abject poverty of all —

that of knowing
only one world.

Activists, lovers —
don't just entwine your bodies,
but also dreams.

When you sleep together,
go all the way!

SIDE EFFECTS MAY INCLUDE

Warning: these poems may cause
headaches, hives, hard-ons in women,

vomiting, vagueness,
feelings of camaraderie where none exists,

false hope, poor judgment,
loquaciousness, perspicacity,

inexplicable tenderness,
sighing, whining, ragged breath,

narcolepsy, excessive nostalgia, smugness,
auditory hallucinations, unmanageable hair,

in some rare cases (under 3%)
lycanthropy has been reported.

Do not read these poems if you are pregnant
or nursing without consulting a doctor first.

AT THIS VERY MOMENT

someone is inventing us.

In the bridal chamber
of the lightbulb,

we are their idea
of a (relatively speaking)
good time.

Profoundly, waves crash
against the molecular shore.

In eternity,
time is the big loser.

Your birth is only the afterthought
of your death.

CLONES COME ALIVE!

Clones no matter where.
Clones no matter what.
Clones come on over.
Good old-fashioned clones —

The very first clone,
And clones of clones,
And clones in love,
And army clones —

Come take your place in the book of creation!
Clones come alive!

PROGRESS REPORT

By trade, a waster
of paper, food,
product, time.

By nature: wasted.

Each month I can hardly wait
to throw my check away.

Technology, we've learned,
should be balanced with human folly
in order to malfunction
in the optimal way.

I try my best to deplete
our planet's resources,
but even so, can't gain the attention
of higher-ups who spectacularly
and regularly waste whole cities,
countries, civilizations
in a morning's work.

My boss remains optimistic,
recognizing an innate talent,
still he chides me for my small-town ways.

ROLE REVERSAL

Stendahl claimed he held a mirror to nature.

Like Flaubert, many readers of *Madame Bovary* exclaimed: "C'est Moi!"

Once reality was dumb and brutish —
in need of art for elevation.

But it's changed —
grown baroque and multifaceted.

Today we can no longer take reality for granted.

Now art is the simpleton.

THE NECESSARY TROLL

Once I thought I saw a lecherous troll gesture loudly
beneath a bridge on a box of jasmine tea imported
from an imaginary country in an undisclosed century.
He was trolling patiently for after-school girls
to give him the pearl of their girlish essence.
The tea was so delicate and feminine — really more
like perfume in a cup than something to drink.
I hated the taste, but enjoyed playing chicken with the troll,
letting my eye sweep his dirty corner without grazing him.
No one knew what happened to those who actually did look.
Some say they turned into spiders and crawled — others that they
aged hundreds of years in a blink. I never crossed that bridge,
preferring to believe that as long as I didn't, everything
would remain as it was on the cardboard box. And regrettably
it has. You see, I didn't realize the value of the troll's slurpy
slobber and its power to transform a common commodity
such as tea into a rare and precious thing.

AN ENDEARING DURATION

A couple pulled a cart a long many years
keeping a nameless keepsake worthy —
the donkey they carried too.

Everyone knew them as yoked
and joked about it in a kindred, suspicious way.

The couple aspired to animalism,
but settled for a comfortable middle-class resistance.

They wore standard-issue sexual,
and complained but rarely about the food.

In tight spots, each shone his and her fluorescent best
saying: "I do solemnly take the multivitamin of your mind."

By day, a nebulous braying began.
By night, a consistent shredding of dice and moons
accumulated with them.

Things continued proverbially.
Once a gypsy, always a gyroscope.
Once a nomad, always a gnome.

In the middle, only the cart remained
wandering between — making them young
and forgetful again.

HAPPY NEW YEAR

Push and pull.
Squeeze through
the breathy bottleneck.

Music thunders
over inconsistencies
of plot.

One often hears
of cheap sentiment,

but of what
would *expensive*
sentiment consist?

I would surround
your words with the finest
of kittens and steeples —

a blood-orange sun
dripping over snow koans
in summer.

There are some for whom
this would be anathema,
but I can't imagine you're one.

THE FOOL ON THE HILL

His hair isn't gold.
His thousand voices fake.
His habit neither young nor old.
His eyes are spinning plates.

But nobody seems to notice.
They can see that he's just a fool.
They don't like him,
The fool on the hill.

Why does he place himself high above us?
What does he do all day on that hill?
I moved away many years ago,
But for all I know he's sitting there still.

Nothing is his buried treasure.
A goose egg is his perfect score.
Zero is his favorite hour.
Zero the revolving door

That keeps on turning
Round and round and round.
Woah ooh,
Round and round and round.

From this fool I learned a lesson.
One thing on which I can depend:
Foolishly, the day begins,
Most likely foolish it will end.

CLICK AND CLONE

Heartbeat-
       flipbook.

Clonebooth.

            *

Caught in the layer cake
of an ancient argument.

            *

Syllabic
Silhouettes

            *

(between)

lunar parenthesis

            *

morning &
evening grids

            *

Spirit construction
workers

see-through
dimensions.

*

See you womorrow —
or maybe Satyrday?

*

Surf's Up!

brainwaves

*

Green
Mother
and Child.

Green
Rocking Chair
Earth

*

Love —

I have put on
this ape suit for you.

SOME QUESTIONS MOVIES ASK US

What if I first saw you, a vacancy sign in a storm?

(Your hair dripping headlights)

What if I moved unaware of the surveillance camera?

(Clutching my incognito snacks)

What if accidents *never* happened?

What if you could only rescue one toy from the fire sale of childhood?

What if a clock were ticking under every word we said?

What makes giants barbaric?

Who can read misguided maps?

Can an entire civilization die of boredom?

How is it Romans always have English accents?

Why were so many Indians white?

INSTANT PAST

I like a certain shade of lipstick because as soon as I put it on, I feel older. Not in terms of years, which would hardly be a selling point, but as if a distant, more glamorous past suddenly appeared.

Yes, that's my mouth. I recognize it, but I'm speaking a peculiar staccato dialect of roofs piled closely together along a river. I'm not sure where I am, but I'm in no hurry. My voice is smoky and lazy and trails behind me as I go.

I have a job in a cabaret; a boyfriend who waits tables, throws knives, walks a tightrope in his sleep. It snows often here, which makes my mouth glow, inviting as a glass of kirsch. And the war is always going — still going on — like music in the background.

I surmise that my problems in the present amuse she who is me in this version of the past. We are two different women joined at the lip by a single color, observing each other in the full moon of a tiny mirror.

"You don't know how it feels," is what I think she says, "to have a whole country pulled out from under you. History happens fast!"

THE POLITE ONES

have stolen my identity.

Robbed me of my naturally
murderous vitality
with their cagey emptiness.

Oh! I will smother them
with this turquoise cushion.

Mash it against
their perfectly outlined
crimson lips.

But later I will apologize.

HURRY THE FUCK UP

C'mon, you can walk a mile
in fifteen minutes — one-legged.

Now get going.

AMIDST A FROTH OF FERNS

Three shrunken heads
planted in a window box.

WHY I READ NIETZSCHE

the slow arrows of beauty

the snowflakes of malice

the fifty worlds of alien ecstasy

gruesome and sweet infinity

Venice as another word for music

cynicism as the highest thing achievable on earth

soul flutes

neighbor love

the drop of graciousness under dim and thick ice

EVERYBODY HAS DREAMS

Last night, the cook dreamt a giant mouth dribbling blood
or ketchup. He has trouble relating to women.

The woman in the beige pantsuit dreamt of a computer that
transports objects into the future.

The woman by the window was a little girl holding her mother's
hand.

That guy near the door followed a melody into a forest.

The busboy was driving a sports car fast.

The skinny girl was a military general in a country ruled by a giant
inflatable cat.

The waitress murdered somebody. Even now, she looks guiltily
over her shoulder as she wipes the silverware clean.

NEW CULT IN TOWN

I lose my flip-flops in the restaurant.
Come home — bare feet dirty.
When I open the door, there's a shiny new bathroom
(unexpected) on the first floor of my building.
Some guy I've never met says: "Feel free to shower."
"Thanks. Maybe another time."

"Who's that?" I say to Jerome upstairs.
"They just moved in and they worship the Earth," he says.
"They gain all their power by lying facedown
  in the dirt for hours on end."

"Oh." Turns out I know two poets who also do that.
  But a third warns me not to get involved —
  that they're kind of skeezy.

A SUBLIMINAL WOMAN

lives under my tongue
without words.

Never center.

Always the frayed edge,
grainy scratch,
slow dissolve.

A woman who's seen
too many ghosts.

Dusted in flour
like a fish.

Her dark eyes,
on occasion, gleam

as if to say: "Buddy —
I *am* in your dream.
No mistake. Take a good look
and then forget it."

Just this once.
They always do.

(   )

I'm lost.
I teach somewhere.
I'm late — no, early.

There is an altar,
but no priest.

A stage,
but no speaker.

No mediator.

I'm tired.

There are some nice colors —
orange and greenery —
geometric shapes.

The floor is a mandala.

I walk slowly across
the holy game board.

I'm speaking. I already spoke.
I'm waiting to begin.

A famous man is supposed
to be here to share his wisdom.

I teach somewhere.
I'm lost.

LED ZEPPELIN REVISION

That stairway only leads halfway to heaven.

THE NEXT LEVEL

These days we're often called upon to perform really wanting. To look with steely, misty intensity into an imaginary camera and declare: "I really, really want this. I am so ready for this. I don't even want to think what's going to happen if I don't get it."

One problem I sometimes have is that I'm too old to really want anything that much. By and large, really wanting is a young person's game — one designed to separate the well-above-average from the insanely overqualified. Still, I'm willing to try, if that's what it takes, to rally the collective force of my unmet needs.

Yesterday, I decided to start small and practiced really wanting a ham sandwich. I visualized it — slick, thin, pink slices piled high. I ordered it on rye with mustard. There was no Plan B. When the cook handed it over with something of a flourish (perhaps he sensed how much it meant), I carried it off like an Academy Award, basking in the why-didn't-I-think-of-that looks of envious fellow diners. It was a moment of unambiguous triumph and made me realize I'm not entirely opposed to playing the really wanting game.

I can see where it could be useful to have that information about yourself, to be able to distinguish wanting from really wanting. Compared to really wanting, wanting is almost like not really wanting — in which case, why bother?

However, before I commit to a totally passion-driven life, I want to consider the downside. If you're trying to decide between, let's say, a two-hundred-dollar camera and a two-thousand-dollar camera, really wanting is key. But for going after complicated, long-term goals, it's likely to prove more a hindrance than a help.

For one thing, it clouds your mind, makes you melodramatic when an analytical approach would work better. For another, it requires time and energy that could be more profitably spent in diligent study or practice. That's why I've decided, for now, to limit my really wanting to either things I can easily purchase or things for which I have absolutely no aptitude. Lack of talent in a given area does not preclude really wanting. In fact, it allows you to focus on it exclusively without becoming bogged down in realistic details.

Yes, I think I'm really getting the hang of this really wanting it. And with each step that brings me no closer to what I desire, I'm able to perfect with a casual shrug, like those existential, anti-heroes of old, that other skill so crucial to our present society — that of not getting.

MY LIFE WITH FLOWERS

Cast of Characters

Elaine, a writer who loves flowers
Paul, a florist from Thailand

Elaine: I've always wanted to write a book called *My Life with Flowers*. Wouldn't that be great? It could be about you.

Paul: No, no, no. I see flowers all day. When I go home I don't want to think about flowers. *My Life with Flowers* sounds awful!

PYROKINESIS

Cast of Characters

Jerome, a poet with light brown hair and glasses
Elaine, a poet with medium brown hair and contact lenses
Martine, a poet with dark brown hair and glasses

Jerome: Pyrokinesis is when you look at a person and they burst into flames.

Elaine: I'm the opposite. I look at a person and I burst into flames.

Martine: When I look at a person, they turn into water.

Jerome: I try to avoid looking at people.

POST SONNET

Sniper 'toyed' with cops
School driver forgot tot
Canary cop is caged
Docs pin 'hops' on rabbit

Korean Ka-Boom Looms
Embalming Fluidity
Chorus of Worry
Wife dies in flat-fix tragedy

'Madam' stays in big house
Lethal home swindler sobs her way to jail
Dept. stores sales rise from the dead
Suspect blows as kin take stand

Rock 'n' roll gets old
We'll always hate Paris

DAILY DOUBLES

for Harry Crosby

Inside Info
Runaway Banjo

Silver Knockers
Too Much Zip

Checkered Rose
Winter Prayer

Tsunamic
Pink Viper

Brave Sir Robin
Not on my Turf

Danceland
Defrizz

Imagistic
Street Bird

Valid Notebook
Perusal

Renovate
Boxitup

Cute Cognac
Milliondollar Moon

Cool Days
Dirge

Planets Aligned
Sure You Can

LOCKET WITHOUT A FACE

The name *Equi* means *horses* in Latin.

While growing up, there was a racetrack at the end of our street.

Evening coincided with post time.

Darkness arrived with the flourish and fanfare of trumpets.

During heated races, one could feel even from bed the tremor of the crowd on its feet.

The smell of horses was not the least bit unpleasant.

The jockeys wore bold patterns: diamonds and stripes of warring colors.

Green, white, and black vs. purple, orange, and gold.

There was something medieval about it. There was something abstract and modernist about it too.

Being a child, I rarely went to the racetrack.

I stayed in my room and studied a box.

There was a girl's face in a heart on the box. I think it was bubble bath.

I knew without having to be told that I was supposed to insert my face in place of hers — imagine it was me trapped in someone else's heart.

But by then, I had already developed the habit of trying to see through pictures.

Whenever I looked at photos, drawings, ads, or paintings, I always tried (like Superman) to see the other side — even if it was just blank.

My life at that time seemed bound up in looking through the locket-shaped window like a telescope into a more feudal age.

Inside the box were things I liked: a penknife, a bar of soap in the shape of a flower, a green plastic mermaid, a fuchsia paper umbrella, a blue glass shell. Insignias, emblems.

These things belonged not to me but to the girl whose face was in the heart.

Or I should say they belonged to me when I imagined myself to be her.

I served her by collecting them.

She served me by disappearing conveniently whenever I opened the box.

A face should not be locked inside a heart.

THE LADY WITH THE ALLIGATOR PURSE

I always knew
I wanted to be her.

A bag lady —
but a rich one.

The singular remedy
where doctors and nurses fail.

Coming and going,
my attaché-totem in hand.

PARTICLES

specs . . .

      dots . . .

           bytes . . .

atoms . . .

      scraps . . .

           snippets . . .

tweets . . .

Some are whole
as seeds contain a whole

galaxy of fruit
and vegetable planets
within them.

But some are missing
pieces . . . flakes fallen off of
incomplete histories,

the way a snowflake
could still be unique
but not quite finished freezing.

Who would know the difference?
How could you tell?

THE COLLECTED

for Barbara Guest

I like the feeling of incompleteness,

the icy *un*resolve
(some would say lack of closure)
in your poems.

A good stubborn modernist
refusal to cohere —

chords and wire tendrils left hanging,
semi-seductive exposed brick of midair.

Abrupt exits and entrances.

Modulated chaos.
Easy-listening for fin-de-siecle ghosts.

Like adding zero to wildfire zero,

sharp thoughts etched fine
then abandoned —

the way one sometimes works
with great energy in the morning
going as far as one can.

Are words thought
or afterthought

or something in between
that evaporates yet lingers?

A poem is made of words and spaces —

but can the fiction of words and space
exchange places?   Switch off and on

in fields of bright decoding,

the selvage of blue
remnants worked into unfinished sky.

DESIGNER GLOOM

Many people have a taste for ruins —
a desire to breathe the rank and fetid perfume
of decaying flesh. Corpse Breath bottled
in elegant crystal flasks. But ruin today
hasn't the proper time to decompose itself.
Scandal is too swift; the new overtakes
the not-yet-old. There simply isn't room
for a sagging cathedral to melt into a puddle
like the wicked witch. Nowhere is there a poet
who sings the sanitized decadence of our times.

A WOMAN TRAPPED IN AN AEROSOL MIST

I live in a clock in a corner of the future
beneath its glass gears and weightless weight —
in a room I share with numerous holograms,

space being at a premium
and privacy (as we know it) a thing of the past.

They are a strangely violent breed —
beefy and spectral — these agents
whose identity is never made clear,

who look like bouncers but claim to be florists
and mask their aggression with flowery speech.

Not everyone can see them either.
Some know them only by smell.

A WOMAN OF THE WRONG ALTITUDE

Turbulence. Bad posture.
Air pressure falling
in the cabin's head.

Islands lost somewhere.
Oily velour below.

Idle among
the industrial
music set to nonmusic.

Panic like a playing card
turned suddenly face up.

FLUTE GIRL

Every symposium needs at least one.

ANTIQUITY CALLING

Looking at Mapplethorpe's Polaroids, I learn that he
liked shoes and armpit crotch-shots of men and women,
both shaved and un' — all giving a good whiff to the camera.
But best of all are his pictures of ordinary phones
which convey a palpable sense of expectancy as if
at any moment, one of the fabulous, laconic nude men
strewn about might call. One could pick up the receiver
and hear the garbled sound of ancient Greek and Roman
voices reveling in the background. But even when silent,
the dingy phone is a sex organ — cock asleep in its cradle.

A START

The
     silver
         hour

drops —

a spider
on the mirror.

    *

Silver
the hour

like drops
of a spider's
mirror.

    *

The silver drops,
the spider's hour,
the mirror . . .

AUBADE, LATE IN THE DAY

for Thom Gunn

The boy gleamed.

O tall, well-dressed
young buildings —

does he live here
among you?

THE LIBRARIES DIDN'T BURN

despite books kindled in electronic flames.

The locket of bookish love
still opens and shuts.

But its words have migrated
to a luminous elsewhere.

Neither completely oral nor written —
a somewhere in between.

Then will oak, willow,
birch, and olive poets return
to their digital tribes —

trees wander back to the forest?

READING ISABEL ALLENDE'S *THE HOUSE OF THE SPIRITS* OVER SOMEONE'S SHOULDER ON THE SUBWAY

and again

the mute song of the windows

seeing her to clarity

READING SANDRA BROWN'S *EXCLUSIVE* OVER SOMEONE'S SHOULDER ON THE SUBWAY

"Because of me," Barrie said forlornly.

"I don't buy this 'seclusion' nonsense for a moment."

READING J. A. JANCE'S *INJUSTICE FOR ALL* OVER SOMEONE'S SHOULDER ON THE SUBWAY

1.

"What about the chicken?"

"Oh, for God's sake Beau, lay off that chicken."

2.

        left home
        go back

So
Not completely.

All
        the rest

        an antiquated system

        a permanent place
        in the Bunglers Hall of Fame

48

READING SCHUYLER

His gift was the ability to see buildings bloom
in unusual, at times theatrical light.
Flowers were memories pressed between
the thick pages of skyscraper books.
Their fragrant speech he understood telepathically —
or just liked looking at them   silent   naked.
Weather was clothing — i.e., a spiritual scarf or hat
one threw on mornings or evenings.
Books were closest to him of all. The voices
in his head. Those dead but still true.
Drugs were facts. No getting around (without) them.
His colors make us hungry: "What a paintjob, smooth as an eggplant."
He could say: "A cardinal enchants me with its song" and get away with it.

SIGHT UNSEEN

It's been a long time since I looked into anyone's eyes as if I thought I'd find an answer, some truth, a window (how silly it sounds) to the soul. Not that I don't believe in souls — only that they no longer reside within us. Even if coaxed with music and drugs, the soul is shy. More shy than the naked body is the naked soul. Lenses, X-rays, MRIs, surveillance cameras, panopticons, our obsession with sight has made us blind to the invisible. And then too, everyone has had to become so skilled as a performer. Even animals act their parts, looking appropriately cute or feral. The eye, once so potent a symbol, a gateway, says nothing, seems corny. Now the only eyes I like to look into are the eyes of certain actors in old movies, for they shine as if imagining, like the religious zealot, a world no one else can see.

COLLECTIBLE TEARS

Pear-shaped tears on greasy cheeks.

Thin, trembling chihuahua tears.

Fashionable, glue-on rhinestone tears à la Man Ray.

Watery tears, cloudy tears, viscous tears thick as porridge.

Musical tears worn only to the opera or symphony.

Hundred-proof tears of high alcoholic content often passed
from one generation to the next.

Lacryma Christi: the tears of Christ. Not only did he turn water
into wine, he cried champagne!

Masculine tears thought to be more rare, and as is often the case,
of higher value than feminine tears.

Wedding and funeral tears, too common to be of much interest.

WHAT IS IT ABOUT HANDS?

1.
I never think of them.

They do their work automatically.

Mine are small and childish — almost paws.

I'm not "good with them."

Once when I was young, my mother burst out laughing
as she watched me try to sew a hem.

2.
Wait, now it comes back to me —

my obsession with hands — not real ones,

but the hands of statues and mannequins
with their perfect fingers and polished nails.

They seemed to reach out —
"a spare pair" from another world
offering metaphysical assistance.

I bought one from a street vendor
who had a whole array of artificial limbs
spread out on a blanket.

How I loved that hand! Would hold it shyly
when alone — and kept it on my coffee table
to add a surreal touch.

But some girls I worked with came over for drinks
and stole it. I remember calling them and feeling rather silly saying:
"I know you've got my hand and I want it back."

Them giggling, then finally acquiescing.
It wasn't the same though. I looked at it differently —
not knowing where it had been.

SOME THINGS NEVER CHANGE

Once I had a body

always tired
of pretending
to be me.

Now long gone.

Replaced by files, codes,

a social network
held together with pins.

The reach of its reach
(you wouldn't say arms)

much further
but still, tired.

ONE CLONE IS TOO MANY AND A HUNDRED AREN'T ENOUGH

Did Poe's protagonist, William Wilson, end up killing his double —
the one he thought was always mocking him? I forget.
And what about Dostoevsky's double? Didn't that guy
move to another country or something? At first,
it may cause problems when there are more than one of you.
People tend to take sides and favor one over the other.
Your shadows are always stepping on each other.
In the past, there was a this-life-isn't-big-enough-for-
the-both-of-us feel to it all. But now everyone is so busy.
No one really cares which one of you shows up.

EVERY CLONE NEEDS A BACKUP

in case something misfires.

You don't want to put yourself
through all that trouble again.

In the future, when people get married,
they may routinely make up another mate or two,
like a spare set of keys.

And then divorce will be different too.
"My ex got the house, but I'm keeping the clone."

We may even look back fondly to the time
when there was only one of everyone.

Not like this trend where people die
and you start seeing them everywhere.

ON HOLD

Sucking on the pacifier of my iced tall latte.

*

White butterflies: flying lint.

*

My tattoo reads: Whatever you think I'm doing, I'm not
doing it.

*

Sticky self lugged around.
Poison monopoly mouse and trap.

*

O.K., let's meet at Duane Reade, but this time use my
name.

*

After years and years, it's finally dawned on us.
Art is not an object, but a way of looking at an object.

*

That's a real Chucky painting.

*

Only 39, 38, 37 more steps to the Holy Grail of Ice Cream.

*

dog days
kerosene breeze

cartoonish faces
heckled by light

*

My hair doesn't do stringy. Frizzy, yes; stringy, no.

*

tamales! tamales!
orchids! orchids!

torchids   ormales

*

Are you feeling super imposed on?

*

Three heads are better than two.

*

Autumn Mutability
Drip-dry Rain
Net of Dust

*

We've had this lack of conversation before.

*

Please be patient. Prayers are being answered in the order
in which they were received.

CANCELED FLIGHT

I.
How many days,
    nights has it been
        without birds'

flighty upheavals,

coquettish bird-bathery,

flashing their blatant *V?*

Birds that sing in Chinese and Sanskrit,
how slowly I walk without them.

2.
Into what other zone,

other story, other poem
have they flown?

In what other city
do they hatch
their birdbrained schemes?

The trees go on
as if nothing has changed.

3.
Remember how the moon
would flap its silver wings?

There were more stars too.

The sky was always busy
behind our backs
teeming with gods and angels.

Maybe birds never existed
or only in ancient times like Homer's.

I am trying to draw one from memory.

It has rosy cheeks,

      a galloping heart,

the rest — a vague softness.

4.
Early in summer,
I dreamt they fell out of the sky
like the first drops of rain.

Planted themselves
      upside down in the earth,

strange flowers
brewing trouble,

wings, a pulpy fruit.

And now — not even a feather.

5.
ex-cardinals
ex-pigeons
ex-robins
ex-finches

ex-starlings
ex-sparrows

expatriate birds
that shit on sentiment
and refuse to ornament
our lawns

ex-nightingales
that pause midsong
for a very, very long time

faster than thought
can cross a blank sky

FROM BUMFUCK

Time oozes.
Ideas (what few there are) fester.

I'm stuck in the lowlands —

the scrub,
without my bottle of bleach.

Another poet took it,
then pretended to know nothing.

The day before, I lost my wallet.

Was sitting at a reading in my underwear,
looking for a pair of socks.

When my turn finally came, everybody had gone.

"What happened?" said the MC.
"You emptied the house."

BACCHUS

Wayne Koestenbaum has written a book
of captions and photos called *Rome and Me*.
I'm looking through it and it's pretty funny.
Later, I'm trying to sleep (in the dream!)
and a guy with grapes on his head keeps
jumping on the bed. I start to snarl at him,
but then I'm like "Oh, I get it — you're Bacchus."

A BING CHERRY MASH NOTE

Black juice —

the first
of summer —

from fruit
made fruitful

in the mouthengine

ORANGE AND BROWN
DESTINATION

Like sitting
in air-conditioned fire.

Antlers sprout
from glowing walls.

VOTIVE CANDY

1.
Give us a sign —
O Lady of the Lemondrops

2.
Betty & Lucy
cherry & orange
call & response

3.
Color is a kind of armor

4.
blood-song in the sugar skull

5.
People say: "Go with your gut,"
and you have no idea what they mean.
Today won't be like that.

6.
Practice the slow calligraphy of summer

7.
Gloat and Gleam

8.
sucking the venom
out of the lollipop

9.
Crystallized melon
served in honor
of Richard Brautigan.

10.
Life begins
in the jelly bean
gene pool.

11.
licorice night
above the lacquered
swirl and fray

12.
I can't see . . . I don't know . . . it's hard to say . . .

13.
Hi from the Witch's Mall!

14.
My country, 'tis of thee,
sweet land of lunacy

15.
pinwheel racers:

teal spirals
on cold steel

16.
unfurling a new flag

17.
Glazed tiles of
apricot and plum,

poison vials
of cordial syrup

18.
Count them all by morning,
and the princess is yours.

19.
(even elves make mistakes)

20.
Somewhere between
three wise men and three stooges,
an epiphany comes.

21.
Pessoa writes:
"Look, there's no metaphysics on earth like chocolates."

OXCART PRAYERS

I try *not* to think as I speak them.

(Ghosts can read minds.)

Sometimes I visualize a sticky, sweet
sunset that fades.

But mostly I let the words carry me
past office-graveyards,
wherever (I'm not particular)
they happen to take me is fine.

KEEPING QUIETLY

watchful through the blindfold
of sevenfold darkness —

the doctrine of Manifest Density:

1. bright darkness
2. cloaked darkness
3. clotted darkness
4. the dark gong
5. the humming dark engine
6. the plush cinema
7. the disco bat-cave womb

TO EDDY POE

The original man in black.
It suited you well.

Living on bread and molasses for weeks
in Virginia with Virginia and Maria Clemm.

Feverish, hungover —

your job as content provider:
to add a literary sheen
to the "fashion plates, music, and love tales"
that comprised the early magazine.

Interjecting them now and then
with your own bloodcurdling hue,
unerring sense of what would set
the public's collective heartbeat racing.

There was always a beautiful woman dying in your mind,
refusing to stay in one grave for too long.

Up and down the East Coast in a stupor,
from Boston to Baltimore you followed her
and were yourself followed by that crazy bird
of ill repute that brought such fame.

"Nevermore" becoming a catchphrase —
something witty for actors to say
or for you to whisper in salons and saloons.

When the lights were sufficiently dim,
the ladies would shiver on cue.

Forever perpetuating its own finality —
even as a child, it was your favorite word.

LOVE SONG FOR AN ENEMY

I love you
but not enough

to kill you
or let you live.

Such indecision
cost me years of sleep.

My mind
full of doubts
like geese.

One day of reckoning
I'll have a secret rendezvous
with indifference.

Step back
while you pass
like a cloud.

A GUIDE TO THE CINEMA TAROT

#1 THE TERROR
(Jack Nicholson gets washed ashore)

If you open your mouth
the sea will rush in.

If you eat a cupcake
frosting will stick to your nose.

Keep your ear to the ground.
I mean all the way down.

Listen.
The dead have something to tell you.

#2 THE TIME MACHINE
(Rod Taylor reassures Yvette Mimieux)

I know you're afraid of strong feelings,
hard work, and hairy men.

I myself am afraid of apathy,
atomic weapons, and propaganda.

We're both adults, but adults can do crazy things — like start wars.
And Nature can turn against us too.

Sometimes, it's good just to talk about your fears.

#3 THE TIME MACHINE
(Yvette Mimieux surrounded by flora and fauna of the future)

Your hair may look strangely puffy today.

Use extra conditioner
and make an appointment to have it trimmed.

Later, let your eyes do the talking.

#4 THE GIRL CAN'T HELP IT
(Jayne Mansfield unbuttons her blouse)

Marilyn Monroe wasn't Jean Harlow.
Jayne Mansfield wasn't Marilyn Monroe.
Anna Nicole Smith wasn't Jayne Mansfield.
Thankfully, there is only one Britney Spears.

But know, whoever you are,
whatever your gender, hair color, physique,
within you there does reside an unhappy blonde
archetype with enormous breasts.

It is her you need to contact.

#5 BLACK ORPHEUS
(Eurydice offers a word of caution)

Know your limits
and stay within them —

in a bamboo room
with a bamboo curtain
stirring slightly between us.

#6 THE MOON-SPINNERS
(Hayley Mills has a question)

Ask.

But ask as if you were an adolescent girl.
You're more likely to get your way.

#7 BLACK ORPHEUS
(A guy in a skeleton suit parties with dancers in Rio)

You're only as dead as you feel.

#8 SWAMP WOMEN
(Two female inmates in Louisiana decide to take their chances)

The guards are asleep.
The alligators just ate.
Go!

#9 BLACK NARCISSUS
(Deborah Kerr looks pissed)

Don't argue with an angry nun.

Eventually the abbess
will throw herself into an abyss
and you won't have to deal with her again.

#10 FIRST SPACESHIP ON VENUS
(A female astronaut is on a mission)

Today is a day to take control.

This missile, this helmet
fits like a second skin.

I'm at ease in them
and can project
my naturally timid nature
without fear —

see myself in the mirrored cloud
sexy protective shield
of my sister planet.

#11 CINDERFELLA
(Jerry Lewis sleeps in)

The wicked stepmother will just have to wait for her breakfast.

#12 THE MOON-SPINNERS
(Hayley Mills gets chatted up)

Like a jewel thief —
that's how smooth he'll be.

Expect to find yourself at a wedding soon.

#13 THE MOON-SPINNERS
(An English tourist tries to keep a low profile)

No, you're not being paranoid.
Someone really is after you.

#14 JOURNEY TO THE CENTER OF THE EARTH
(Science penetrates a steamy cavern)

reishi, shiitake,
enoki, morel,
porcini, peyote,
oyster, chanterelles —

get friendly with a fungus today!

#15 BLACK ORPHEUS
(Orpheus knows a good thing when he sees it)

Search everywhere for beauty.
When you find it, whistle.

Don't get stuck on cute.
Don't be pacified by pretty.

It's harder than you might think
to see for yourself, but keep looking.

#16 WHAT A WAY TO GO!
(Gene Kelly isn't about to disappoint his fans)

Dive into the mosh pit.
Be collective in your consciousness.
Wear the perfume of a crowd.

#17 THE 7TH VOYAGE OF SINBAD
(A diminutive princess gives good advice)

Heed the small still voice,
        blue fairy,
        inner flame.

Pay attention to details.
Take one baby step toward reaching a goal.

#18 THE MAGNIFICENT SEVEN
(Yul Brynner and a friend brood over drinks)

Those who live outside the law
must adhere to a stricter moral code
than those who simply obey it.

Use your powers for good,
and one day they'll name a robot
in a theme park after you.

#19 THE MYSTERIANS
(Two stylish space invaders address the people of Earth)

Others see you as exotic —
often imperious — a diva
"from another planet."

Try not to make everything you say sound like an order.

#20 THE MAGNIFICENT SEVEN
(Robert Vaughn keeps up a good façade)

It's true, you're slipping.

Not as quick or charismatic
as you used to be.

But we still love you
and wouldn't want you
to do anything heroic just yet.

#21 SAYONARA
(Marlon Brando can't help looking like a winner)

Confidence brings victory.
Victory brings confidence.

You're caught in a vicious circle of success.

#22 SAYONARA
(A geisha plays the role of Spanish cowboy)

Don't just cross-dress —
while you're at it, change your ethnic identity too.

#23 FINIAN'S RAINBOW
(Petula Clark holds a high note)

Follow the path of a song.

#24 THE MOON-SPINNERS
(Eli Wallach and Irene Papas disagree)

I guess it's no surprise
your family is against you.

Expect a roadblock
from someone close to home.

#25 THE MYSTERIANS
(Arrogant aliens strut their stuff)

Go ahead, conquer the world.

When you walk by
all the giant dildos
under sonic bell jars

in the great hall of sex toys
start to twinkle.

#26 JASON AND THE ARGONAUTS
(Hercules and a shipmate wonder whether or not to plunder)

The chance to walk away with a fortune
has you in a sweat, but it's not what it seems.

Avoid get-rich-quick schemes.
Spend time at the gym instead.

#27 THE MOON-SPINNERS
(Hayley Mills focuses on an object of desire)

Never underestimate the power of eye contact.

#28 THE TIME MACHINE
(Rod Taylor takes a spin through the centuries)

You were made for the future,
but don't just wait for it to come to you.

Plan. Project. Set your watch ahead.

#29 FINIAN'S RAINBOW
(Fred Astaire hides his lucky charm)

Make a pot of soup
from gold
and fragrant grass.

Bide your time.
Let your treasure simmer.

#30 THE TIME MACHINE
(Rod Taylor proposes a new theory)

Speculate.
Engage in metaphysical debate.
Reverse the law of cause and effect.

The more heretical your idea,
the more likely it is to succeed.

#31 BELL, BOOK, AND CANDLE
(Jack Lemmon works his magic)

Someone you've always wanted to meet,
possibly a celebrity,
will suddenly appear out of the blue
and offer assistance.

#32 FINIAN'S RAINBOW
(Fred Astaire gets enlightened)

The silent speak.
The elixir is complete.
Equanimity is reached.

This card can't grant
immunity from chaos,

but it does promise
time and gold enough to read by.

TRANSPORT

I'm back in Murakami World. Thank goodness! The i.v. drip of his thoughts is gradually replacing mine. He's more than words, more than sentences — more, in fact, a virtual reality you enter like a resort, a well-run resort where every need has been anticipated.

A fraction of a second before you even know you're hungry, a snack appears. And not just any snack. It's as if a psychic chef had concocted, out of all your quirks and particularities, exactly the dish that would most satisfy you at that moment in time.

How does Murakami do it? No one knows — yet. He is the next step in the disappearing spiral staircase of the novel's evolution. One day his books may become holograms, theme parks, but for now Haruki Murakami remains the darling of creative writing programs everywhere. The man does what they don't encourage — goes outside and talks to the girls with blue and purple hair. Divorced men empathize with his plot: "That guy's wife never did come back. Poor bastard." Menopausal English professors read him and sigh.

Then there's the music. Every novel has its playlist. In Murakami World, life — er, fiction — is what happens between songs. Before he wrote books, Murakami owned a jazz club, and one can still sense the tremendous pride he takes in creating just the right atmosphere.

I get the feeling that once he's chosen the proper record and put it on, the rest takes care of itself. Music is what carries us from one chapter, one world into the next. When we die, perhaps it's not our family that waits to greet us, but our favorite songs.

WHERE WE MEAN

In some places, we are unable to grasp or gather
ourselves. Greasy and grim, unable to ask
in jet-lagged esperanto for directions or help.
In other places, we come together beneath the bare,
black lace of trees. Love is a distinct possibility,
arriving like clockwork in its swan-drawn carriage.
The point of this is just to say what we say sometimes
makes no sense in the countries of different contexts —
that one is, or should, always be testing the ground,
moving a little left or right before starting to speak.

EMERALD CITY

after Wilbert Harrison

I'm going to Emerald City, Emerald City here I come
I'm going to Emerald City, Emerald City here I come
   They got some crazy little wizards there
      And I'm gonna get me one.

   Well I might take a plane
I might use a cane, but if I have to crawl
   I'm gonna get there just the same.
I'm going to Emerald City, Emerald City here I come
   They got some crazy little wizards there
      And I'm gonna get me one.

PINK CHRISTMAS

for David Trinidad

Once again pink seeps in.

The rose door is ajar.

In the pink cubicle,
pink ghosts are loosed.

Pink pirates navigate
the deep magenta seas.

Under a necklace of icy lights   ,
a trio of pink ladies
sip Pink Squirrels studiously.

They are my pink Alma Mater.

Pink completes the crossword puzzle.

Pink sands shift
in the dunes of memory.

HAT ON A PILLAR

A fuzzy girl's hat
perched rakishly
atop a svelte
column of concrete.
A gray beret,
angora oyster —
abandoned, askew.
The girl who wore it lost
herself or turned to stone.

DIGITAL SKY

I think it should be orange today
with maybe just a wisp of purple
hovering there above the cathedral
that was once a disco that will soon reopen
as a food court. Sometimes it takes a few minutes
for it to drip all the way down and cover us.
And we take these pauses as free gifts.
Time fallen off its timeline — the sweet
but brief kiss of an anarchist before
everything resumes its picturesque.

THE TENDER TRAP

Yesterday they were playing Frank Sinatra at the bank. Not soft background stuff. They were blasting big band Tommy Dorsey classics like a pizza parlor or the small branch of a newly opened casino. I took my money from the ATM, half expecting to see a row of slot machines nearby. That way I could give the money back before I even got outside the door. The bank has been gradually changing its image. Since most transactions are now done online, employees with nothing better to do often loiter in the entrance greeting you like a high-school friend and asking about your weekend. They've put a huge dish of peppermints and cinnamon hearts by the deposit slips. They give away baseball caps if you can guess their latest interest rates. It's all very cozy and carnivalesque. Although, I vaguely remember a time banks were formal, almost somber places because taking care of money was thought to be serious business. Recently I've heard of a bank with a Starbucks in it. Maybe soon they'll add a buffet, a boutique for selling designer sportswear. Why not a floor show? As long as it's not a poetry reading. A poetry reading in a bank — that would be going too far.

HE LOOKED LIKE JESUS

But the Jesus who liked to party. Jesus with a devilish side. Not Madonna's new boyfriend, Jesus. More like sixties-hippie-Godspell-Jesus-Christ-Superstar Jesus. Jeffrey Hunter with a dash of Charles Manson, who often claimed he was Jesus, thrown in. Skinny, pale, long hair, beard, glassy faraway my-kingdom-is-not-of this-world eyes. I imagine he must get a lot of action — lots of people wanting to get saved. If he's tired of it, he ought to cut his hair. I assume he's an actor (no one could have a face like that and not try to cash in), but maybe out of work at the moment. Not much demand for Jesus in movies since Mel Gibson has fallen off the wagon. I wonder if he has a girlfriend — a boyfriend — if he can walk on water — change water into wine. Where's he off to? I could almost follow — except what if he walked into a church?

I THINK OF THOSE NIMBLE SEERS

so adept at side-stepping
hordes of multitudes, crowds of signs.

Willing to act as interpreters,
they became the translators of one century
into the more rapid speech of the next.

Eternal bachelors —

married to no tradition,
settling on neither side.

I wonder if there are any like them
here   now.

READING LINDA HOWARD'S
DEATH ANGEL OVER SOMEONE'S
SHOULDER ON THE SUBWAY

If she'd had her place

      enigmatic.

          Annoyed

If she wouldn't have seen him at the truckstop,

if he hadn't kissed

READING MEESHA MINK'S
THE HOOD LIFE OVER SOMEONE'S
SHOULDER ON THE SUBWAY

Destiny says:

    "Surrender

      motherfucker!"

          *

              candy-apple-red

              we go way back

READING ROBERT L. VAUGHT'S *SET THEORY* OVER SOMEONE'S SHOULDER ON THE SUBWAY

Proposition 1.2

Assume A, B, C

> *Often one compares U to*
> > *(among numbers)*

as laws in the theory of switching

> *Great*
> > *important*

Finally, there is another better analogy.

THE MORNING OF THE CLONE

Day opens on a close-up of grass and trees
vibrating in that miracle growth solution we still call rain.

While in their cells, monks copy long columns of DNA.
It is tedious coaxing the nucleus from memory's tiny speckled eggs.

To see without my point of view — be me without myself to blame.
And to do this work continuously. No one has ever been

so unoriginally free from sin. I sip my usual iced tall latte
and take it in, this world forever ending without end.

Destroy. Dismantle. Delete. It remakes itself without
missing — no time anymore for the old farewells.

E N V O I

Go, clone — tell them I tried, but not enough,
that I was overly fond of lingering, unable to adapt.

Say it in my own words — now yours.
"One substance and one colour."

See those places I was too lazy to see for myself,
that I preferred to imagine as distant, foreign.

Find him, clone,
that fabled other "braving time."

Confirm for me the rumor
that somewhere difference still exists.

A BOWL OF SNOW

1.
Into the plaid mountains, children vanish carrying books.

2.
What will anyone remember about today?

3.
To an ant, the frog might as well be a dragon.
To a chubby girl — o.k., a prince.

4.
Changing the Lightbulb:
Let brightness welcome whoever enters.

5.
zombies out on a cakewalk

6.
midnight in the church of face-to-face

7.
My Problem

First it was the size of a mouse;
then a worm.

But it's still a problem —
and now it's loose!

8.
Dumb-show:
I know (at least I think I do)
something — but mustn't let on.

9.
In the center of every word is a picture.

10.
Pictures can cure us of words.

11.
"There it is — the rocket of Johnny-ness!"

12.
All writing is a kind of bookkeeping:
Ledgers of who said what.

13.

You've got to think there were at least one or two spiteful
scribes who in setting down their master's words decided
to alter them a bit. Even the Bible ends with what's
basically a tamper-resistant seal — i.e., curse on anyone
who changes anything.

14.

There is a door in this wine that leads straight to summer.

15.

A premonition of peach.

16.

Easy to sleep late behind a beaded curtain of rain.

17.

Dreamt I edited an anthology called *Animal, Vegetable,
Mineral* that tried to capture three different speeds of life
(like old record players).

18.

A) I should have taken a pill.
B) I shouldn't have taken a pill.

Most days it's one or the other.

19.
Pregnant with blankness

20.
I operate better in the fog.

21.
"Here's the part where all the broomsticks come to life."

22.
Magic makes visible what's already there.

23.
Homer invoked Athena,
Sappho — Aphrodite,
Milton — the Holy Spirit,
Hopkins — the Virgin Mary;

I wonder who I can get to help?

24.
A Near-Perfect BLT

The bacon is great;
the organic tomato really steals the show —

but I'd make the toast just one shade darker.

25.

Twilight of the billboards.

26.

They live in a Garden of Word-ly Delights.

27.

How'd you learn it —
which buttons to push and all?

28.

Used to be every poet signed off as Orpheus.

29.

You Know the Type

A NY guy
in a NY hat
walking a NY dog

30.

Sorry but you are talking to the wrong ghost.

31.

My Year with a Pet Rock:
Keep it up and I'll marry it.

32.
How dare you answer me as if I were an e-mail!

33.
She maintains the aura of the drone.

34.
The Sun's Resume

I am cheerful, reliable,
and haven't missed a day's work
in over 4.5 billion years,
give or take a few hundred million.

IMMORTAL CIDER

How many cereal boxes, cans of tuna,
by light of your clear mountain flute?
In the village of my village —
mind polished, meat like mist.
Can't stop a mirror from looking.
Can't stop a heart from tying useless knots.
Vines climb a green and twisty stair,
daily rewind their journey of a thousand steps.

NOTES

"Why I Read Nietzsche" is a list of my favorite expressions by the Ubermensch himself.

"Post Sonnet" is comprised entirely of headlines written by the consummate poets at the *New York Post*.

"Daily Doubles" uses the names of horses taken from the starting line-ups at Aqueduct, Meadowlands, and other well-known racetracks. It's dedicated to Harry Crosby because he particularly enjoyed the sport of kings.

"Reading . . . over Someone's Shoulder on the Subway." I've always enjoyed reading over someone's shoulder. There's something so intimate about a person absorbed in a book. For several months whenever I took the subway, I shamelessly indulged this fetish in the name of found poetry.

"A Guide to the Cinema Tarot" began as a photo project that involved making my own film stills from favorite fifties and sixties movies and then writing short poem/fortunes to interpret each one. I intentionally created this piece so that the visual and writing components could be appreciated separately or together. Within the poem, I give brief descriptions of the photos, but as is often the case with much ekphrastic poetry, I don't feel the reader actually needs to see them.

"I Think of Those Nimble Seers" was inspired by Charles Baudelaire.

Special thanks to the Genetic Science Learning Center at the University of Utah for permission to use *Click and Clone*, the title of their ingenious and educational website (http://learn.genetics.utah.edu) as the title of this book. To my mind, it captures our Zeitgeist in a way that is both witty and succinct. Of course, any views expressed in these poems in no way reflect theirs.

ELAINE EQUI was born in Oak Park, Illinois, and raised in Chicago and its outlying suburbs. In 1988, she moved to New York City with her husband poet Jerome Sala. Over the years, her witty, aphoristic, and innovative work has become nationally and internationally known. Her last book, *Ripple Effect: New & Selected Poems*, was a finalist for the Los Angeles Times Book Prize and on the short list for Canada's prestigious Griffin Poetry Prize.

Among her other titles are *Surface Tension*, *Decoy*, *Voice-Over*, which won the San Francisco State University Poetry Center Award, and *The Cloud of Knowable Things*. Widely published and anthologized, her work has appeared in *The New Yorker*, *Poetry*, *The American Poetry Review*, *The Nation*, and numerous volumes of *The Best American Poetry*. She teaches at New York University, and in the MFA Programs at the New School and the City College of New York.

COLOPHON

Click and Clone was designed at Coffee House Press, in the historic
Grain Belt Brewery's Bottling House near downtown Minneapolis.
The text is set in Iowan Old Style.

FUNDER ACKNOWLEDGMENT

Coffee House Press is an independent nonprofit literary publisher. Our books are
made possible through the generous support of grants and gifts from many
foundations, corporate giving programs, state and federal support, and through
donations from individuals who believe in the transformational power of
literature. Coffee House Press receives major operating support from the Bush
Foundation, the McKnight Foundation, from Target, and from the Minnesota State
Arts Board, through an appropriation from the Minnesota State Legislature and
from the National Endowment for the Arts. Coffee House also receives support
from: three anonymous donors; Elmer L. and Eleanor J. Andersen Foundation;
Allan Appel; Around Town Literary Media Guides; Patricia Beithon; Bill Berkson;
the James L. and Nancy J. Bildner Foundation; the Patrick and Aimee Butler Family
Foundation; the Buuck Family Foundation; Dorsey & Whitney, LLP; Fredrikson &
Byron, P.A.; Sally French; Jennifer Haugh; Anselm Hollo and Jane Dalrymple-
Hollo; Jeffrey Hom; Stephen and Isabel Keating; the Kenneth Koch Literary Estate;
the Lenfestey Family Foundation; Ethan J. Litman; Mary McDermid; Sjur Midness
and Briar Andresen; the Rehael Fund of the Minneapolis Foundation; Deborah
Reynolds; Schwegman, Lundberg, Woessner, P.A.; John Sjoberg; David Smith;
Mary Strand and Tom Fraser; Jeffrey Sugerman; Patricia Tilton; the Archie D. &
Bertha H. Walker Foundation; Stu Wilson and Mel Barker; the Woessner Freeman
Family Foundation in memory of David Hilton; and many other generous
individual donors.

NATIONAL ENDOWMENT FOR THE ARTS

This activity is made possible
in part by a grant from the
Minnesota State Arts Board,
through an appropriation by the
Minnesota State Legislature
and a grant from the National
Endowment for the Arts. MINNESOTA STATE ARTS BOARD

TARGET.

To you and our many readers across the country,
we send our thanks for your continuing support.

Good books are brewing at www.coffeehousepress.org